The mirr

Also by Michèle Roberts

A Piece Of The Night
The Visitation
The Wild Girl

As co-author

Touch Papers (*poetry*)
Tales I Tell My Mother

The mirror of the mother

Selected Poems 1975–1985

by Michèle Roberts

Methuen

A Methuen Paperback

THE MIRROR OF THE MOTHER

First published in Great Britain 1986
by Methuen London Ltd
11 New Fetter Lane, London EC4P 4EE
Copyright © Michèle Roberts 1986

Printed in Great Britain

British Library Cataloguing in Publication Data

Roberts, Michèle
  The mirror of the mother.
  I. Title
  821'.914   PR6068.015/

  ISBN 0–413–58790–8

for Monique and Reg Roberts,
my parents

Some of these poems have previously appeared
in the following magazines, collections
and anthologies:
Angels of Fire; *Apples and Snakes*; *Bête Noire*;
Bread and Roses; *Certain Gestures*; *City Limits*;
Cutlasses and Earrings; *The Left and the Erotic*;
Licking the Bed Clean; *The New Statesman*;
One Foot on the Mountain; *Only Poetry*;
The Politics of Spirit; *Smile Smile Smile Smile*;
The Third Eye; *Touch Papers*.

I'm grateful to many friends/poets for
their encouragement of my work over the years.
I want to thank the following poets
in particular for their valuable criticism:
Alison Fell; Judith Kazantzis; Sarah Maguire;
Chandra Masoliver; Ann Morgan; Ann Oosthuizen;
Stef Pixner; Tina Reid; Diana Siminonds;
Michelene Wandor.

Contents

The mirror of the mother

the monk
stands
under a flowering tree

prodigal with sweetness

women come women go
and come with earthen pots
to fill his, thus their own
torn flesh of priestlessness

lacking substance they
subsist on his
spare shadow
stain his robes
which burn with sacrifice
to make their merit
                   food
and beggar both they give
men and children suck
for their salvation
                   their
coin of vile body
seeds the ground
                prodigal
with sweetness

under a flowering tree
the monk
stands

the women of the harem

the women of the harem
over breakfast
compare dreams

I was the cup of water
in the desert which he
drained the piece of glass he
wore as diamond the sand
that sucked the fire of his
flesh the silk
that wrapped
the blood of his
bed the oil of
pleasure for his
still limbs I his
casket he my
drowned key

divided angels
swoop
and gobble dry stones

everyone saw me
flashing in the distance
I was a rock of strength

I was such a good baby
I never cried

my tears now
squall every rescue fleet

may my tears be
green rain upon my rock
a flood to rock me
out to sea

pirates learn
to use the pilgrim's coracle
mothers wear cutlasses
as well as earrings
we are teaching our children to swim

caterpillar

she births herself, the grub
the woman eating fear, her
bones black and prickly
tunnels the dark, a dream of water

she weaves a house of hair
golden as Marilyn Monroe, scornful as Hippolyta
sweetness glues her mouth, her angry tears
polish her jet-black coffin

she lives the night, the moth
splitting herself open like a rifle-shot
she straggles out, dusky
and brushed with brilliance

she whirrs above the forests
by day she hangs in men's houses
sometimes when still
she fears her largeness and her loneliness

she conceives while flying, the woman
balanced on blades, her art
is to construct what is possible

her daughters' hundred feet
fly in the face
of what is called natural

when holofernes slept
then it was
that judith slew him
with his own sword
by her hand

when samson slept
then it was
that his strength left him
his own hair
by delilah's hand

before you sleep
I shall come before you, wet
and naked utterly, our
own bodies shall be
our pavilion, you shall not
need to wound me
to escape

then
o fearful lion of judah
see
I shall take your sword
into my mouth, I
shall lay my head
inside your mouth
samson carrying gates is lonely
lay your hands upon
my gates, grasp
my hair, bury
your sword, your fingernails
clotted with sweet wax
taste
the honeycomb
between my lion's jaws

judith returned home
married and bore six sons
became perhaps
an intolerable shrew
delilah at sixty
still has to
dance for a living

he keeps himself inside a
no, sorry, he's a
no, that's it, *yes*:
he's got a

stereo
a motorbike, a library
a pair of jeans, and so
he's not
into things
he can't relate
to women who are

they just cross
and tangle
his mind

he lustens to the rodeo, the sweet
mewsic of his own
spheres, he tames motorbooks
ejokulates the Word
into chamberpets, and wears
his blue meanies
with a tight
lip

he can't relate
to women who are

Klevshaven

(Norwegian for 'Cleft haven')

this is a different country
the first night I was here

I was dry before I came
your lips parted to show me water
a spine of fur and molten sun
you called me across oceans
come to klevshaven

your house soaks me in sun, waking in
your bed at the heart of a marigold
your walls are white
I blink against them, lizard
in your hair's noonday

men and women built this landscape
bulldozers and lunchpails, gardens and funerals
the sun and aeroplanes twist above the river
when the sun goes down I smell your darkness

I wanted to slide further into you, klevshaven
and to suck your forest and hear your waters
crash in our silence, and to show you
the delicate mosses that grow there

my woman friend of ten years standing
those ten minutes when I lay beside you
were crammed with the riches of a life

there can be no rest
we have often parted before
we know we shall always
visit again

you stared across the mountain ridges
of my hands
it is better to sleep now
my house accepts you in a different way

the rocks keep cropping up, boulders
piling in layers along the road
push at our talk of books and food
indefatigably monstrous, yet
their insides whorled as simply as sweets

I will suck them to swallow them down again
at night they are fluorescent and make me sick
each night the mountains
swallow your sun, and my dark sun
burns at noon in a snarl of gulls
to jag my flesh with my flesh

the woman in me is huge now
you are too close to see her perhaps
her pines scratch you instead
she rolls over carefully, her thighs
laid about the river, awaiting
her work, the explosion
to whorl her insides as simply as sweets

the attic is mine now, here
we gossip, our mothers' ghosts
their photographs and account books
recipes, patchwork
sobs and gestures
boil behind that door

nothing has changed
you said, you see?

you who are wise, you know
plenty gone mad in flowered aprons
the screams in aspic, and desire
bleached out on mondays
you who are wise, you know
no herb will heal me

when I am from you
I shall not be dead: the fishbone
child who had choked me
swims on my words now

a woman is fighting
not to be mermaid
calling you softly, klevshaven
klevshaven, klevshaven, women
have landscapes to build, men and women
have landscapes to build, to build

the child dreams on the way:
this is a healing time
the earth turns
over and over
under the comb of ploughs
lines drawn inexorably
deep as the backbone
her body shudders
further than fences, her
limbs lit
and releasing sun
acres of pale stalks
flush with pleasure, she is my own
mother and harvest and hill

next morning the father is out
early and picking
penises in the field
innocent pink
flesh gleams in his fingers
the mother sleepless last night
plunges her hands into water
her eyes rooting through glass
for meaning
between
and the swell in the field
only scholars can talk
to that dead goddess in her tumulus
the mother's anger brings fruit
crashing from trees
she does not like sudden
movement loud noises
the child was raised in the freezer
the child is still yelling
their meals are anguished
they want, they want

the train moves the woman
even farther away
until the next time
cows tuck their glossy knees under
they accept their place
glazed in the sun
I am not porcelain
never to shatter again

he wishes he were a
one of those able to
dance and shake
breasts and belly and hips
loose, a
not-himself, nothing-but

he wishes they did not have a
hiding from it in his bed stillness
he bruises easily

he wishes he were still a little boy
so that he did not have to face them
telling him he is an oppressor
he needs them to scold him
darling oppressor

if he were a
he would join the   movement
but at least his   friends
are always   who struggle

he has nothing to do but
help them out of
silence, he has
nothing else to do
with   oppression

he wishes they had a   too
so they could all just be friends

Lin's death

(for Lin Layram)

she's going to die
they all say so
the doctor the dietician
the faith-healer the psychotherapist
all have departed
she calls herself a terminal case

the cancer creeps firmly on
like a hole
singeing in paper
her hair turns grey
she is tiny, hollowed and burnt

Lin we danced together
in street-theatre days
you were Poodle, pregnant and glamorous
you juggled, waved feathers and sang
not much makes you laugh now

you still move amongst us
your name is death, death, death

when I touched your hand
in the cinema
I feared it would crumble to dust

her funeral

(for Lin Layram)

she died in the middle of winter
the sky was grey-faced
and the roads were blank, all
trains and technology halted
we journeyed towards her death
stumbling in snowdrifts
our tears were icicles

the hearse was late, lost
in whiteness, the unmapped fields
while we waited at the end of the
long lane tunnel, in the village church
we prayed to the chilly radiators

her father-in-law tried to comfort us:
let not your hearts be troubled
she is merely sleeping
she has gone before us
she will rise again
her body will be glorious and new

in the churchyard I saw
such a little, specific box
such a deep, such a little bed

her husband and friends
lifted her, as they were used to do

under the cellophane and snow
the flowers were very fresh

in the light we climb the mountain
called the Old Man
blue snow, dry, freezing, gives
my feet inch-holds
my boots dent his white head, I
grind rocks together, laughing

we sledge at midnight
eyes open upon the dark
only my sick stomach jumping
tells me one fall ends
another long
rush begins, my
muscles clench and bang
the hurtling alley of my fear

here I am
whooping into darkness, back
beyond, way beyond
puberty, blood out of the unnamed stone
plunging towards the woods
and the frozen lake they fringe
its hidden cavern, body-shaped

the sledge crashes
my cheek rips along
the water's rigid face
black ice scathes my spine
my eyes would poke the stars out
if they could

luminous, loading
more than half the sky
the Old Man floats
solidly

filling all that space of
loss, black loss, sweet black
with omni-
present white

I labour up the glassy slope
to start again
practising letting go

mother, letting you go

I have been wanting to mourn

I have been wanting
to mourn for a long time
to mourn for a past time
the bells of the ambulance this morning
beat at my head like angry fists
beat up my heart if I let them

in the French village of my childhood
each death, a steeple
rocked with our grief
so we assembled, we knew
who was meant, the bells told us
a clang for each year of the life
the black copes of the priests
blotted our bright tears
we sang rejoicing, God
had eaten another of us, we were still
his obedient children

years later, in England
relatives began being
ticked off at Golders Green crematorium
meat out of the fridge
and into the fire
we prayed, our lips
stiff as the corpse
we were too young to see

and there have been friends
three of them
dead by suicide
I have hung their carcases in my throat

I want a funeral first
where I can mourn
mothering, and mourn me
losing and lost, I
wanting her cradle, fat
gobbler of gaps, my consolation
the grave shovelled into my mouth

I have found women
to witness my loss
of blood, of mother, of childhood
called puberty (that is all —
the word should be larger than that)
I call myself woman, I try to

no one can ever love me like that
nevermore
no never again

therapy 1

the site is old waste, raw
planks press the dust
metal bits tinkle and jam
weeds in a high tide
slap at a rubble beach

clear all this
build me a house, I want one
bright, cool as a palace
big as a fun-fair

suddenly you say
you are no architect
you have no plans
there are no props

words, I whisper, I shout
are Trojan horses: the thief
in the night to the other asleep;
words are walls: I am besieged
and must defend

words, you say, are touch
are stepping-stones, images
exchange of gifts
words can be food

I'm all over the place
tough, sneaky, dogged
as Menelaus, Ulysses, Hector
and Paris, I'm
those chums in drag, a
pantomime beast with three legs

you are like Helen
only in this: your
beauty, your
patience, your
other loves besides me

cooperation, you say
no more plunder and pirating

inside my armour, I melt
as this, my long
my dangerous war ends
what I fear now is the plain
outside the city:

love's wrestle
and peace

Daphne to Apollo

our confusion, to make men sound like gods:
unnatural woman, you are a tree
fixated, lost, with a deep gash
to be rained upon, rubbed up against
hidden in, struck down
sold, and burnt, your ashes
worthless

I plead, I can twist like metaphor
I approximate, I sway knee-deep
in ferns, I am cultivated, lovely
my bark is a thick plait

I rear myself near a woman lover
we are the hedges around farms
the milking-stool, the cradle
we furnish ships and boxes
brooms, coffins, desks, and paper
we are your floors, your windows
our roots nourish us, twinned
labyrinthine memories, between us
passages, and gaps, and halts
the darkness wet beneath
the perplexed canopy of our hair

my father carves his name
on each in the plantation
clears our flowers, strips us
in a single word
I have stooped for years
I have smiled around him
now, when I fall upon him
crushing, still he protests
you are my tree, only a tree

I too have words now, I have words
I am a woman in the city
but my dreams
flower with him

the forest is long ago, is
deep coal now
I pace the labyrinth
following the gold plait, thick, and knotted
when I find her, I am not only
heroine, but also minotaur, she too

memories of trees
who never yelled, or wept
or went away

punkrock; and Cocksparrow sings

I didn't expect it
(I like to know
what will happen, control it)
times have been hard, we were tired
(no you never get what you
want so don't
ask; if you are good, in fifty years' time
the revolution will give you
a book of instructions)

we went out dancing
in darkness, in glitter
an anniversary of sorts:
two women
six months of hard loving
hot little communion
with ninety others, your hands
root me, swaying in stars
your face, brighter than neon

I am sixteen as never then, fascinated
by sweat and satin and beer, the band
raucous, young boys on the dole
touching and innocent, yelling
mother, we are *so* bad, please
take us home
they hate the audience which
consumes them, their rage, their despair
I confront them, brazen
belonging: my hand in yours

back home to bed
you touched me gently: this could be
your benefit night
suddenly
you lay there laughing, your hand
leaping at me: come on
woman, come on; I flew
up and down
twice, and I came, it was simple
as that, I was amazed
and delighted, so proud
of myself, I didn't expect it
such prodigal
opening, such ease, and such
celebration

my bit of power
you never sang of, Cocksparrow
I compete with you still
last night I tried to forget
our separation, our
loneliness

I am abroad in a strange land

I am abroad
in a strange land
loving a man again

I thought: this
is the capable man, broad
bones and a frame for
lifting; he knows
words and
winds, combs seas, views far
where the marsh sags
where the stream gobbles
the forest's hem
he will join hands
to make me a path across

I thought: I'll be the gentle field
waving with grass and smells
where he lies down, I'll be
his summer, his
scarlet poppy drug to
soothe him, he will suck
my silk, my wiry stem

it grows dark
now: the winter afternoon
smears light with mud
the sea dashes against a fragile wall
the forest's gone, grey into grey
the marsh sedge waves and sighs
a single heavy mass
alive with goblins
shrieks of sudden pits
the track through fear
too narrow for my single eye to thread
he's gone, he's lost
and therefore I am also gone

he loses me, he flails
a broken windmill in the sky
he names me as the storm, me
as the grabbing marsh
I shake, I hide, I name
him as the hunter, he
shoots my violent woods
my knocking sea

when we search for one another
winds muffle our words
we must call loud, and hard
our feet inch the chaotic earth

the eldest son goes home

these are his bones
of his flesh is this place made

the house grips him
with the teeth of love

silk beds are flung for him
game slaughtered, at his mouth
whole generations
of feeding-bottles held

their gaze upon the woman
that he brings is cold
her hands divide them
name her a whore: she goes
easily
naked and wet for him

his mother calmly dotes
on china figurines
his father bays and nags
to whack his penis off

while her man sleeps
the woman walks
she hangs upon a fence
watches the windy rooks
she tosses like a rag
on ploughed horizons
under lines of elms
barer than they
and very small

the house behind
belches, and smiles
and licks its maw

she feels alone so much
two nights of sleeplessness
can't shut her eyes
upon the homeward train
through the dark country
and the suburbs limps
her hero in his nasty dreams
he can't remember how
she fought for love of him
he carries cases up the chilly steps
she mocks her pretty skirt, she wants
to stick a hatpin in his eye

of her bones too
her flesh, and these two days
are children born

I have just come from the war

I have just come
from the war
I ducked about
like an ambassador
between contestants
with my pretty face
I jabbered on and on, I offered
anything for peace
lies kisses gold

it's an ill wind
that blows nobody
any good change
this wind blows on

I toss, fuss, protest
I was a liar when I said
with clocks, maps, calendars
I was life's gaoler –
now, there is only this wind

once I was a fat baby
once I was a star
once I was the teacher's darling
once the king chose me for his bride

now, far away
mothers wave farewell flags
now, tiny
triangular jewelled jets
draw you through tropical nights

plants take their time
and seasons, and embryos
waiting for birth; I want to force
maytime, a bloodied spring
and your return

this wind blows on
I am rebuilding my house
after the war
and with you gone

I bruise myself on him
the rock man, parched, reserves
himself in case of further drought
he remembers ancient storms
he is fragile and he may break
my tears erode his base, my
blood spatters a fastidious peak

I burn myself on him
the ice man, far away, preserves
rich gardens under snow
and memories of mummy, her enormous lap
my heat drives wedges
to his anxious skin, my clumsy feet
precipitate an avalanche

I starve myself on him
the skinny man deserves
no less than this: I have become
harpy, snatching in the night
I have become wind, tempestuous
tossing, a home-brewed hurricane

I have cut off both breasts
and I will not
no, I will not

the vicar's wife's song

only Christ is my lover
whom I forgive
much: my misery, his silence; my
beauty is all for him, I shut
hooded eyes, my pale face
haggard
jerks with ecstasy and with irritation
at a filthy oven, at the eucharist

I bawl from wall to wall
my curiosity and my tense endearments
the tiny cardboard house
boxes my lust as dues for Holy Week

I should have been born
in the time of Teresa
or Joan, I want
splendour and style
I am ashamed of that

meanwhile, my husband, the clergyman
smoothes his hair in a separate room

he dons gold drag and smooches with God
I bully Jesus, I have
no peace

the mistresses' song to husbands

together two
cities tremble
         between
dark and glitter
bounding tensions pulse
                our
filthy hands sustain
your lace
     and prick
         your
newly laundered smile for
wife
    whose boulevard of green
and iron frills you
tread for sunday pleasure
                we
your rich and necessary closet
mulch your oratory where nuns
as blue as sugar-bags ferment
the slum with prayer
            flesh
boxed in spikes our hungry gut
strings twist against your
mouth
which tastes
our cargo grown
in backyard
colonies

having hooded my face with hair
having hung, all night long
lips apart, over a silent pit

having crouched, having borne down
and down, having yelled
having delivered myself

having danced, having bitten
cloth, beaten air
until the song came

having delivered myself of a strong song
I collapse, gasping, with dissolved bones

she who came to me, she who called out loud
she who licked at my ear
like flame, and sank in
deep as a wound, she who swelled in me

she whose winged breath
wrestles with mud and
shapes it to pots and houses
she is my lady, she is the secret word

having lain with many men
having remained virgin: unmarried
having loved women, having shown
forth my big belly, my songs

I shall burn for this

I will sing high in the fire
oh let the fierce goddess come

nightshift

up there
men and gods collide
down here
the night is black
with stars
                Orion
the Warrior
straddles the street

I drag my dirty linen
between his legs
into the space-age
launderette
nowhere to sit
                    our
heads and legs
bow to the heat and wet
mouths busy
rinsing experience

my neighbour
stuffs a hundred
pairs of underpants
into the colour telly gone mad
kicks the door shut: ain't you
finished yet? come
on man, machine, ain't got
no time to waste

a final shudder
the white foam
spurts to the drain

later I lie
between your legs
upon clean linen
my laughter stains your white night

you insist
there are obsolescences:
hands that once curved over clumsy tools
carve chips in silicone, compute and clock
brain galaxies, cosmos of nerves and blood

soon, you sparkle
language will wither away
like wings on fish, binary counts
become collectors' items
like masculine-feminine, couples
and jealousy, we'll throw
new switches in the unconscious
and polka to the dialectic
of the paranormal

oh but you stir me up
you curvet in a colt's entrechats
whirl to my arms like
seeds that september scatters
fall, thudding like fruit
onto my earth, albeit
wishing to renounce
custom and gravity

civilization's acrobat
I dare you to include
these atavistic surges of mine
these sarabandes of the woman corsair
this centuries-old
collapse and cry

norfolk weekend

we swallow the air like earth
the sky is a delicate wall
on which we paint with clouds

the orchard stoops and drops
dark pink
apples in the long
grass, little
fallen sunsets in
green twilight

the land is pegged
with churches, five
on the horizon
but it still flaps brown
and stony

far across the field
the blackbirds chatter on
and red barns hug the earth
trees whistle for fled blue

blue tiles, blue roof, blue
dark sky

death dons an apron
death stirs the pudding
death lets you lick the spoon

death rocks you
when you wake from nightmares
crooning: there, there, baby
don't cry

death takes your gifts
and props them on the mantel
death spoils you, death
dresses you in paper skirts
for Christmas pantomimes

death has wept so long, so often
death's breasts are withered
death takes medicine, death is bitchy
death laughs, death dances
hola death

death sits alone
and stares at darkness
death remembers
death is not polite, she burps and gossips
death says: God
gives with one hand
and with both hands
takes away

death, teach me your songs, your stories
let me hug your wisdom
one last time
death embrace me, death sit next to me

death oh my loved one my grandmother

red-haired lover

only your hair is on fire
beech forest tucked
under my chin's hill

blue midnight blankets you
curled small in my skin's cave
white reed of flesh
pale lily of juice

you spill your secrets' seed
all night
you grow me:
a giant mama-gourd

sometimes your red sun
rises in me

the spring is unbearable
the wet sun spatters
the smashed
house of the snail
and the hyacinth hurts and hurts

the birth of brawny weeds
their riotous assembly
rips apart
my pavement skin
that lovers tango on

oh my mouth
aching
and bruised by light
my eyelids
violent as plane leaves
in the dark rain

my waist
bends and bends

sap oozes, rises, bursts
in me
and runs
fresh hollowing tears

I holler at the moon

the big man

I want to spin you, big man
make you skip
hop, twirl on nimble toes
I want to whip you like a top
my tongue lashing you
with ropes of silk
till you unfurl
flags, flowers, parasols

I want to be a crazy blackbird
singing all night lewd
riddles to your smiling ear

won't you make my blood
jump? won't you
step along up there
clowning and glittering
beneath the big top, and
see me stretched out here
your fine strong net
with nothing on but jewels?

boom! go the drums of sweat
as neon bodies wink

big man, you hold me in your hands
big man, you warm me with your tender flesh
I am a bee hauling honey out
a fly tickling a slow fish

the clamped bud
splits, green armour clangs
down, raw scarlet silk
flares like a parachute

the petals' mouth
those red doors
the way in

stamens and pistils burst
up, each sticky velvet brush
gold pollen glistens on
their black fur tips

deep winy heart
as dark as raspberries
for plundering wasps

translucent sun-traps
colour running like a hot
streak of shiny sweet
juice in tossing cups

season of passionate red
opening, red
festival of flames and tongues

lullaby

you're the night watchman, fingers swimming
cloaked along dark streets, you spill
lantern light on flesh, slow
guardian of my city's
deepest cellars, round and round you go
you're familiar with my doorway
every hour this summer night
my cones of lilac burn, and drip
like candles, you call out
all's well, all's well

you're the nightingale
you're the cock at dawn

you're the bruiser, boy, you lust and leap
you scale your mother's lap
like hills in el dorado, leave
home for ever till tomorrow
when she lets you slip, and slaps
you swarm up apple trees, steal fruit
rip legs off flies

you're the pirate baby
you're the mouth at the sweet wine

you're the night fisherman, you push
long finger boats along canals
you slide, exploring, in between the river's lips

and you're the man
who pleasures all my locks with oil
who has the key, who knows the way
in, and who hears me call
all's well, all's well

wine rages in my blood
a tight red crown

the car noses
down tunnels of trees
lilac drifts against the darkness
splashes of black
on a black dress

I wake all night, from blue
shimmering dusk to blue
bird-bawling dawn

I watch the leaves uncurl

you have gone away
at last you have given me leave
at last you have given me notice
of all your absences

the sky is my sheet
my night is odorous
you sweet corpse leaping
over my wall

she is marvellous
the bosom, the nose
uplift satiny smooth
brown jelly
sweep of the hair
rollicking forties curls shine
sausage-rolls ribboned on top
the paint smiles
all the time
her fingers tap, tinker
with glass, cigarette, compact
her eyes
dance on tables, her feet
twine, pompom mules
pink powdery spikes

her man yawns
I want to scream
as I wait
get her out of here

the arch of her foot
dark, like a grey breath
cherry suede bridge, shoe
binding flesh in
red-patent, snappy bright bars
tender tickly constraint

he picks fruit, she feels
delicious
flurries of pain

I have been
stuck on your spike
I am not sung
like Christ or Sebastian
I am a doll, merely, of paper
pending
impaled for reference, I am
fixed
by my deepest heart

you call this act love
I embrace a pillar of dread

she lives alone
normally
it's tidier, it takes so much time
scraping off those
pollen drifts that seep
through window cracks, excising
mushrooms splitting the eiderdown

she lived in the jungle once:
hard sun, the
bite of green, wet
pools and writhing ferns
dappled shades where people
screamed, tore flesh
on rocks, fought in the mud
they touched each other
and themselves
continually

she remembers her parents gardening
him pulling up her mother's flowers as weeds
he smothered her wilderness
with crazy paving

Lizzie's walls are firm now
her backyard is cemented over
at night she crouches there
waiting
for the first, tiny
heads of weeds
she smashes them
she smears their vile juice
with her spade's edge

a jungle yelling at her windowsill
she has no refuge anywhere

the first task was to persuade them
a woman could go
that my heart could and did ring
like warrior drums
that I could curtsey to dragons
and then slay them
that I could leap seven leagues
at the drop of a high-heeled boot
my mother and father complained
there was no farewell ritual for me
but I had brand-new disguises
and I needed to go

the second task was to search
in a dark wood for years
alone, and afraid, and not knowing
whether I touched
men, or gnarled trees, or hobgoblins
still, I learned songs, and the way of the wild
and the wise witch showed me
the way out of the wood

the third and hardest task
is letting you search for me
through thorns, over glass-topped walls
past siren music
and the sleepy drugs of flowers
I must stand still, I must wait
wet, humming aloud, smelling
sweet, smelling strong

certainly, I have few words
and no tricks
for this

sadists use coal-tar soap
they cut their hair like lawns
they eat whole libraries before breakfast
and their bowels are more regular
than first-class parcels

you can tell a sadist
by how gentle he always is
how rounded his vowels
and how twinkly his sweet blue eyes
behind plate-glass specs

more specifically, a sadist
wants you and you alone
first he hooks you
with some sidelong melting glances
a shy boyish smile and
a mysterious allusion or two
to how he really, but no
he couldn't possibly

then
when you've just written a poem
he'll tell you art is neurotic
then, when your friend's just died
he'll whistle loudly in the bath
then, when your heart's
stretched bleeding on the bed
he'll pass you the marmalade
(he won't stop your mouth *with* kisses
but from)

so I suggest you try sleeping
next to a hyacinth in full bloom
so I suggest you try leaving for Paris
with a very good friend

he is merely
socially inept:
the only woman he loves
was never
and is never
there

what started out as a simple adventure
soon attained the quality of a myth

(women are less reliable than men
and somehow, it is usually the woman's fault)

not just the stiff father
frying to death in a costly tin can
— his wife is a radio
sinking cold knives through pink papaya flesh

(paradise is fatherlessness
paradise is brothers and sisters only
paradise is not-words
and not-difference)

not just their swaying procession through green
their bodies flashing like fish in pools
floating like birds under blue and green suns

(we keep making men grieve
when they want to play with us
we are thinking of sunburn and sleep
when they paint their bodies for us
when they dance and wave yellow fringed flowers
we are worrying about birth control)

but he, who quickly became
less and less of a stranger
who would not want such a guide?
male, but not hostile
my love is comely, and black
he is savage, and smiling, and kind

(and what was her puberty rite?
she refused to grow up, she feared what that meant)

being a woman, she knew that it couldn't last
she knew that she needed
streets and shampoo, that she would have to be picked
when the right time came, by the prince
— her black friend blew it, not knowing the rules

(poor prometheus, poor adam, how will you bear
to go through it all again?)

now, in the real world, grown-up
in the city, before her husband's kiss
she sucks on lipsticked cigarettes
and chops his liver to bits

(the black one's hung himself
silly boy, on the tree of her mind)

you say
colour is clear:
fields lie, little
tucked-up
beds of taut green silk
an orange car comes by
glossy as caramel, colts
kick up their smart white socks

I tell you
look again
brown is brighter than shorn curls
and bronze ditches
are deep with the purple of figs
the hedges' olive mouths
are stained with plums
those forests flush, that
beech-flame interrupts
the willows' silver-grey

only your language knows
where rust ends
salmon, pink begin

I tell you
landscape is truer than you
less curt
and more careless

Magnificat

(for Sian, after thirteen years)

oh this man
what a meal he made of me
how he chewed and gobbled and sucked

in the end he spat me all out

you arrived on the dot, in the nick
of time, with your red curls flying
I was about to slip down the sink like grease
I nearly collapsed, I almost
wiped myself out like a stain
I called for you, and you came, you voyaged
fierce as a small archangel with swords and breasts
you declared the birth of a new life
in my kitchen there was an annunciation
and I was still, awed by your hair's glory

you commanded me to sing of my redemption

oh my friend, how
you were mother for me, and how
I could let myself lean on you
comfortable as an old cloth, familiar as enamel
              saucepans
I was a child again, pyjamaed
in winceyette, my hair plaited, and you
listened, you soothed me like cakes and milk
you listened to me for three days, and I poured
it out, I flowed all over you
like wine, like oil, you touched the place where it hurt
at night we slept together in my big bed
your shoulder eased me towards dreams

when we met, I tell you
it was a birthday party, a funeral
it was a holy communion
between women, a Visitation

it was two old she-goats butting
and nuzzling each other in the smelly fold

New England, 1980

light falls cleanly on the back
step, a square gold puddle
a hot stain

fat feathers glisten: bushes
push up, plump as cushions in the sun

fields blow in long silk tides
 — here is the mystery of grass, the
sun running like a wheel through trees

the hills gasp, and are dry
 — such brittle twigs, bleached
wooden homesteads
with a red
lace porch, a single cow

the moon rises
big and yellow as a whisky sour
in the rainy dark, the song
of cadillacs and frogs

rich children on their spotless campuses
dream of utopia
the next frontier

she strolls in the valley, alone
her ears scan the warning
twanging of birds
her boots plop and suck in the mud's grip

the sky is a cold gold spoon
sun tart and sweet
in the cup of hills licked
clean by the gulp of cows
– at the cup's lip, the foam
and crust of milk, a swell of clouds
and yellow plums; leaves curl
like the peel in marmalade

the world is her mouth
a sour swill of yells

trees scar, and suddenly
redden; bright berries of blood and teeth
hang in the hedge; the bad
baby is out; she
bites through the net; she swarms
free, fizzing; she thunders like bees in a box
maddened for honey, and her mama

her lips clang shut on mean rations:
she swallows the river
and mourns on down, a thin bellyful

Leeds weekend

from the train, the metal jaws
of yellow diggers slashing
red gashes in the earth's flesh
clay curls on and on in wet
silk coils: a disembowelling

from your back door
the electric turquoise glare
of rows of cabbages
their bouquets jut, their tough frills
vein in bluey-green, a mist of ice
each stalk's a solid twist of taffeta

from the hill's top, the valley's deep
crack, filled up with blueberries
red beeches launch, burning, off
the slope, we swim
through their soft showers
on the moss, we watch the beechnuts
burst, their cases flap back
in fours; their pips are black
pearls on cold fur beds

droning about men all afternoon
we wasted all these feasts; my
separate mouth
was open and empty and buzzed and stung

this is the last battleground
their skin is a thin barricade

once, they were rosy mouths at mother's breast
once, they were white milk in a flask of flesh
now that sweetness dries, now their mouths are
stoppered up: the tender leather
of wineskins shrinks
to bags of gristle and sticks

war has boarded their bodies up
and they have flares, not eyes
that burn indifferently
through newsprint, onto our TV screens
no patrol can put that fire out
that consumes their citadel

under their barbed-wire crowns
their souls snarl out:
yellow smears along the walls
they are the holy ones, the lonely anchorites
well schooled in crucifixion, by their priests

wild men, naked, on the blanket
wild women, starving for what
new mothering?

after my grandmother's death

each day is a full
spool, and death winds me in
her foot tap, taps
rocking the cradle

death is mrs moon, death is a spry spinster
I am a thread the moon spins with
and I come reeling in from my grief-stricken dance

the moon puts silver on grandmother's eyes
in her nostrils she puts the cold perfume of death
– moonspider spinning shrouds and swaddling bands

my mother's womb spun me a fine cocoon
spun me round and out, death tugged
my umbilical cord, she grinned
and tied me into her weaving

the moon who eats babies on winter nights
has her dark face, and rubbery hands
but grandmother rescued me
and held me close, she shone
steady for me, then I felt so blessed

then death strode out
trawling, trawling
and grandmother was mackerel to her silver net

the womb is the house of death
and each woman
spins in death's web; as I inch
back to the light
death pays out the bright thread

lament for my grandmother on the day of the winter solstice

woman who cradled me, and made me rise
I am bread, you were yeast and salt in me

sometimes, my grandmother, you were busy dying
and your body became a box of bones
that travels towards the furnace to be crushed and burnt

we have surrounded a rose tree with your ashes
between turf lips you lie compressed
a word in a green tongue

when your hip smashed, fragile bone enduring whole
for almost a hundred years
you consented to darkness

you were dismayed, but you consented to death
with some struggle, and you told me:
there is no heaven, there is just us together here now

you closed your eyes and slipped off
(and I wasn't with you)
you tunnelled down through the bedclothes
prisoner of pain you dug an alley down
and then you cut loose and left me alone

most nights, you told me,
you dreamed of your dead husband
love long lost, and you complained to him:
where are you, lover? where have you gone?

my fists thunder on your breast
the bony gate to Hades and the ribbed boat
that takes your spirit there
I harrow Hell, calling out for you lost in the dark

the resurrection, the incorruptible flesh
how you doubted that, watching yourself slowly die
noting the new frailties, your body rotting
to enrich the earth

where are you now, my grandmother, white-
haired warrior, indefatigable voyager?
your pine coffin was the boat you chose to launch
and death the great water it furthered you to cross

you sailed off with just one bunch
of red and yellow flowers
you huddled in a wooden coracle
and disembarked in flames

you tow me after you
you make me grow on up
and now I am one step nearer to death
and that deep sea
where you rock through the year's long night

the winter enters her
so silent, it
slants in and
squats her; the
thin time of Lent
her skin's a curtain between cold and cold

naked, she fills up with the city snow
and frozen trash; she's a container
for rain-pocked slush and the brown
mash at the gutter's edge; the cold
moulds her, bleak in the park

there's no prince, no melting
kiss; she simply
endures
the dark months
of the occupation, the aching embrace
– like a root

till March loosens her

then there's a white
insurrection
of crocuses; each one blooms
close and full as an egg; how
their purity hurts

she must learn to open her yellow heart

poem on midsummer's day

now is the year's fullness; like
a pregnant bride
she swells in white: the may's
lace tent, the curdy soup-
plates of the elderflower, cow-
parsley frothing like the scum of jam, the
glossy braid and tassels of tall grass

the hill's crown curls with fern
and foxgloves where I lie – blue
views of sloping fields whose ragged seams
are hedgerows deep in green; dark oaks
are parasols for cows; wild honeysuckle
ties the bees in loops

the Mendips shake out lanes
like linen bands; I am born here
dazzled, in white dust, and I drop down
between long banks, the scarlet course of campion
to where sheep squeal, and twitch
their fat rumps at the shears' steel buzz

I am the day's child, I am the year's fruit
now, at last, I am sweetened by sun
after cold seasoning; I am held
in the summer's arms, on a bed of piled warm wool

she's going, the nice girl who smiled
all the time
crossing her legs
her fingertips dipping
at sugar-
bowls and at skinny bread

leaving home, the warm
family smell and the games with mum
— the sky tears in two, grey cartridge paper

on the street
vulnerability lures
like the tang of blood, a single
flick of the razorblade
— of course, she murmurs, of course
I can see that

the new flat, uncurtained, floats
high up and lit; it's
no halo of steel; when she closes her eyes
the noises pad into her bed: such impudence!
on the floor above, a woman
screams rhythmically, and she cannot stop it
nor her lover's curses; their duet is terrible
below: shouts, and shattering glass
a brick? a bottle? in whose face?
next door, a soft shuffle: the avuncular
slippers of torturers

she lies down alone; independence
flickers off-
on, a worn neon sign; she watches the blue
night, bunched like policemen
muscle in through the window; she faces
the dark
beginning again

and so who
was the city's mother? did it
have one? or who
taught the city
to cleanse itself so well?
red buses are licked
clean as a whistle
by starving commuters
tube trains smarter than hoovers
gulp up dollops of junk — whoosh
now you see them — whoosh
now you don't
and autumn streets
which should be flossy with joy
have their deep soft toffee drifts
eaten by yellow machines

no one will let me
come to them
along steps a nimble neat man
very gently he tells me
my open door is obscene

no
the city has only a father
with a gold moustache and a chain
and a stop-
watch for a heart
he made this city, he planned it
his logic laid out squares
as cold as himself
those cocksure terrible towers
those tidy ticketed lusts
he patented them, he made public
his architecture of ice

the moon has been exiled
along with daughters and plants
the moon rocks by in a merry blue flood
the moon throws silver all over me

she says beware

winter sacrament

last night I met my mother again
at the altar steps, in the cathedral vault
we knelt on stone, our chins upturned
we were open-mouthed, awaiting
the body's guest:
the trusty bread, unleavened
delicate as frost

it's a dream, I thought
when I woke up: the street
was absent, a
blank page of whiteness, shops
and cars sunk
under a soft blotter of snow
— tiny, circular wafers of ice
tinkled and whirled at my lips

later, the brilliant moon
in the dark night; cold
and solid as plate
she shone, and her silver hands
dressed the bare trees
— the pavement outside the locked church
was a rink to slip home across

in bed, I shiver and fast
in a snowfield of sheets
lonely for you, my absent guest
our snowflake bodies
melting on each other's tongues
— the true communion

the diagnosis complete, I tried to become
a surgeon, deciding to operate:
I imagined white tiles, a single
whack of the axe, our bodies'
severance, our selves falling
cleanly apart

but rather than simply
rip myself off
from your skin, patiently
I've had to unpick every stitch
that binds us, snipping
at catgut that cries like violins
to the scissors' percussion

thus I expose the wound
red and raw to the february wind

I keep wanting to tell you
how much separation hurts, to re-
entwine, ask you
to be bandage and comforter

this women's work is thrifty and grim:
learning to save myself, learning to live
alone through the long winter nights
means so much unknotting, unknitting
unravelling, untying the mother-cord
– so much undoing

rite de passage

(for Joan of Arc)

it is always the quiet ones
whom the whirlwind picks:
Joan, thrust from dumb worship
of forests, God's fist at her back
the saints articulating
her bones to an iron
syntax, the ringing logic of mail

once she danced in wordless circles
of girls, hands linked, once she hung
leaf-loops, flowers in knots
on trees, her invocation
a green twist, a perfect O

then the vision plucked her away
and sentenced her: the voices
insisted she marry, and name
the new part of herself: war's
rhetorician, she stammered
embracing the angel, faint in his angular grip

Joan, after that meeting
returned to broken places: compatriots hurt
by her eyes'
pure androgynous glare; turning
her face from family, she forswore
silence and mother-tongues

yet, in the end, after victories
after the failed leap from the tower
she was trapped: ecclesiastical
grammar, the rope of deft priests, tied
and tripped her; she conjugated
their only available verb: I confess
to heresy; I am unnatural

they pitied her: duped
peasant, illiterate girl
and duly they sent her back
to the smoking green wood, the sharp tree
– lashed to it, burning, a human garland
poor freak (born too soon) she carried on
crying out messages they could not hear

levelling with death

when it falls from the air
our death will be less
democratic than snow
piling its inches evenly
over hills, hospitals, prisons and palaces

death is no leveller
not any more

death is a ration card
issued by bureaucrats
to the poor, an engraved invitation
to angry women resisting mr
seducer death's burning kiss, prince
charming death's iron wedding ring

next, officer death will stamp
on men who lean to the live
bodies of women, children and other men
with his spiked heel, his inked, indelible boot

dr death has pronounced fit
the prime minister, the army and the police
for their responsible task of sorting out
who is fit to survive the responsible task of
sorting the dead from the dead

death, you spoiled-rotten brat
who will be left to wipe your snot
and hold you as you blub
you didn't really mean to do it?
who will be left to bury you, death?

whose death at easter

(on the train between London and Leeds)

the world container: delicate blue egg
enclosing clouds and air, my bit
of continent a membrane
of sown fields, hairy elms in bud

rivers and rocks quicken and jig
and the view constantly
reassembles itself: a day-glo farm
pink in the sunset shrinks
to a dot behind poplars, the telegraph wires
strum up, strum down
over the railway cutting's fast plait
of brambles that shine in the rain

I wonder which will occur first:
God piercing the egg to suck
our souls out, swallowing
us raw, gulping our goodness down
when our time has decently come?

or those other greedy boys
measuring the nests, to raid them
in cold competition of smash
and grab? innocence
is not in the eggs; they
crush the shells for
certainty, and for punishment

all the sour
goddesses have gone off, spoilt beer
spilt milk, replaced by arsenals of lust

hand in hand, gaily
we invented the wrong God
now we await the terrible spring

1.
how could I ever make a friend
of death? though he behaves
like one: dropping in unannounced

he wears a lover's face, which
touches mine; his garden
smells of rain and summer; here
at night, we sit; he
cuts an avocado pear in half; we
eat green flesh and suck the stone
between us; then we dance; when
he arrives in bed I call it rape

last winter I fled from him
back north to the speechless
waterfall, back to immaculate ice; I
preferred white perfection, I
preferred to remain intact; I sang this
loudly enough for him to hear

this spring my lover
came for me again; this
time my mother did not
hold me back; she blessed me; she
suggested it
was about time; then she released my wrist

my lover is a dark man
we embrace in the garden, in the grave; his
twisting root is clotted with my black earth
as I break open, and take him in

this time no return is possible; this
time he has me; this time when we go
underground we go together
though I shall be crying loudly
for the mother and women lovers I leave behind

2.
in the beginning, I was
carried away by him; helpless; he
welcomed me, and I fell forwards, down
into the depths of him; he
opened up for me; he
made me die, and die

down here it is dark, so dark
apart from the glitter of amethysts
which he breaks off for me
like a flowering branch; he piles my lap
with ammonites, offers me
iron pyrites
phalluses, intricate coral fans

there are days when I shiver at all this
glistening rock he
strokes more kindly than my skin, turn
from his fools' gold, strain
for a lost body, lost light, lost voice

days when my forest
petrifies, and I'm the fossil
woman who resists
his hammer, his chisel, his collector's hands

also there are nights
when his black coal head
lies next to mine, nights when my heart
drums as the twin of his, my breath and blood
in tune with his, learning to sing
of friendship; a difficult, a new
benediction

Demeter has torn off
her yellow linen dress. Its fallen
ruffles drift along the grass.

The beech wood crouches on the slope
dark and shiny; its henna'ed mass
Demeter's hair, which hoods her wet face.

Demeter beats her fists together. Chestnuts
and oaks explode in rhythms of red
pink, russet. Bruises burst on her skin.

Demeter howls: wind cutting the reeds.
Only a mallard shrieks back
here, where the light is watery and thin.

Demeter wraps herself in a black storm
cloak. The afternoon pales, draining
away down winter's throat.

Demeter weeps:
her child's lost
Persephone's gone.

I travel through burning
streets of yellow facades and small
blackened palaces. I measure
the city that swims, the lion city
of carved pink islands and smelly
canals. Every alley leads to his bed.

So many women have gone
down before me into the dark.
Will I plunge up again? Shall
I be born from these water corridors?

Twilight. I am lost in the wild
garden, alone, the swish of chilly
grass on my ankles, night beginning
to coat the acanthus leaves. I turn
and run in a privet labyrinth. At its
heart, a shock: a green room
where the dead
dance in white marble, a nymph shrieking.

No way out. Behind me
in the doorway of cypresses
the man in black.

No use remembering
my mother's walled slope
of flowering orchards, lettuce
and artichoke beds, the bells
that juggle and toss
in a copper bowl held
between the hills' blue knees
the rhythm of her breathing as she sleeps.

Demeter keeps going

(for my mother)

This wood is Demeter's golden house
the sun slaps wet paint on, and
here the goddess tramps about, busy beneath
her skylight of chestnut leaves
yellow and luminous as glass.

She whistles loudly enough
to shake the trees, smiles at the soft
crash and rattle of nuts
into her lap, inserts her fingernail
to split and prise off the spiky husks.

She sorts and inspects her glossy
harvest, the kernels' truth. She
tests each seed with her teeth: sweet
or bitter, the taste of rain or rot
the smell of sap or the sour kiss of decay.

She regrets the spoilt fruit, but
labours doggedly on, stocking the hollow
bellies of oaks. Then, larders full
she packs down leaf mould, rotten
nuts in a compost dance: death is no waste.

She chooses the best of the season's goods
to plant, then squats on the moist
black earth and puts her ear
to the chestnut's bark. She listens for messages
issuing up from the roots, the invisible girl.

Demeter sleeps in her house of twigs
curled under frosty quilts. She dreams
that the coldness will pass, that the barren
fields will stiffen with corn.
She prays that her buried daughter may rise.

She waits for Persephone to return.

Persephone pays a visit to Demeter

Suddenly I allow myself
more than a single room: this year
I explore the whole house, pace
its roof and stairs. All its windows
stand open. All its planks are bare. Salt
lines their crevices. I hear them
gossip at night.

We have restored this house. All
the major repairs are done. Now
we are tidying up, inspecting corners
from attic to cellar. The spiders help us
spinning their webs and sucking up flies.

We lean on a windowsill, looking out
over the estuary and the sea. The sun
flattens the fishermen who crawl across
the skin of the deep. Turning, you display
your newly short white crop. And I
show you my first grey hair.

I'm like one of those boats down there
siren bawling with grief: I'm going back
mother, this time I really mean it
I'm really going.

Persephone gives birth

in the enormous field
tight with corn, the stiff
jostle of stalks, gold arrows
pouring over the hill, heads pressing
Demeter's waist, their heavy tips
cutting her hands that she holds
up and out, hostage
to the harvest and the heat

she beats a path through
she parts the gold waves
she hurries
the cornfield resists

in the churchyard
Persephone in her bone nightgown
squats down

Ariadne: the spider's story

here Oedipus and Theseus
left their trace: these feathered hills
hide monsters

underneath
the scarlet treetrunks
and their load of heavy light
that hangs and trembles
silver-glistening green
beneath
the scorched and quivering flanks
of noon
burn pink and orange bones:
earth, rocks

the holes, the gaps
dryly they show themselves

the mountains shake out roads
like winding-sheets
you could die here, blue-
dazzled as
sour-green hits yellow-grey
these are also the colours of crumpled cars

hulloo, brother, hulloo
perhaps you could tell me why
there is peace in my pink-washed room
stone-walled, where spiders weave;
and green panic that surges
when I'm alone in hot forests
stubbing my toes on stones?

but I forgot: being blind
you'll tell me green means stop
and red means go

here comes a hero now
in golden plate of skin
his beard blazes, both
his swords are blue-steel keen

these tunnels, I tell him, twist
and twine like a woman's hair
these caves are cruel

when he is past, I lean
from the sill of my pink-lipped room
my furry labyrinth
and spin him in

oh pity the monster lady
who must be torn, and slain

after the break-up

on the first day, snow
marks the seams of the fields
smoothly as tailor's chalk

ice wraps the crags
and clings to hollows
the blackness of granite
is spoken in films of white

on the second day
the thaw
the relentless rain

Deepdale melts: the fields
are streams; on the mountain's face
the narrow force
slips down, simple
as escalators, in a whirr of spray

on the valley floor, water's
colours are violent: cobalt
in the grassy pools, rose
over gravel, tartan
of scarlet and jade in the bright bog

after the break-up
small glaciers shift
on the hills' loose staircase
the travelling earth

The bronze cockerels have breast
feathers of blue
steel the sun
has hammered out. Beating
the golden air with scarlet combs
wings, beaks, they bounce
and spring in imitation of the Virgin's
fizz and whizz to heaven
up and down on green turf trampolines.

They are a rowdy
college of cardinals: such red
flounces, such a
tossing of birettas, such a bang
of beads accompanies
their debate of doctrine, such
unholy farmyard shrieks.

While flexible as Jesuit souls
flamingoes tie their necks
in knots, and contemplate
their perfect knees, the bossy
pigeon nuns, the strapping
little sisters of the scrum
knock weaker postulants aside; then
opening their white starched throats
they grab communion first.

A flock of brown Franciscan sparrows
scurries up too late. Deprived
by vows of other consolations
they are blessed
by the bright dawn not
with stigmata but with Transfiguration.

hoarse and heretical
suddenly I'm tempted to join in.

unscientific

morning: he curls in bed, a dark
red bean sunk deep in under
a compost of dreams and eiderdown

all night we are pits of sleep
twin beans, joined
in our cottony pod, skin curved on skin

sun splits the curtains' case, clocks
crack our warm earth; now I await
our green pushes, our scarlet flowers

the fascist, when female, looks
forward to nothing: closing
the window she wheels
back to the dark marvellous room, the
merry-go-round of beds, the
crackerjack jokes, the tickles, the
tucking-up, just one more story of how
the little princess ran away from home
with daddy

the fascist woman is well
versed in chopping brains
kidneys and liver, hair and fingernails
so now she wants
to cut God's heart out
and chew it raw; this way
she believes she can become God

she freezes her tears
in refrigerator trays, bottles
her lust in glass
rows on the larder shelf; her bundle of twigs
is a birch broom: she excludes
filthy rage, the mess of pleasure
by beating her daughter, beating the floor

I know her: when I lay unconscious
last night, she climbed into bed with me
calling my name
she insists we are
sisters under the same skin

he holds his breath

The house rots around him. Three
damp wedding rings on the wall
spell the years of his abandonment.
The facade sheds plaster like dandruff.

He lies, the deserted bride, on the double bed
lapped by dirty shirts, the stink
of old socks. Nightly he vows himself
to the perfect lover on the television screen.

He muffles his mouth with cat fluff, the
feathers of slaughtered birds, and cigarette
stubs. Here, the dead walk at midnight
to the larder, gobble baked beans. He never eats.

He unplugs the friendly telephone, dons a corset
of steel: his ribs tinkle and ring like scaffolding.
The radiators weep. With the garden scythe
he unpicks his mother's letter. He holds his breath.

the oyster woman
(in memoriam Helen Smith)

the corpse filed away in a tin drawer
of the state brain resurrects
herself: a hiccup, a sour taste
on the legal tongue

the pathologist, the surgeon, the policeman, the
            coroner
chew over the meaning of *victim*, of *innocence*
there is indignation, there is gnashing of teeth
analysis shows
there is genital injury, head abrasions
and bruises, which are consistent with rape

their lips kiss the book, will speak truth
her lips are sealed; who kissed
her lips, who tore them?

certainly she was born
and slapped, and breathed
possibly she was drunk
and slapped, and sobered
possibly she was hysterical
and slapped, and shut up
possibly she indulged in sexual horseplay
and slapped his face, certainly she died

analysis shows
the woman on the couch is hysterical
she cries: I am dismembered
I am pulled apart by guilt and knowledge
I cannot remember anything about it
I cannot bear to, I cannot bear witness
I have taken leave of all my senses, I was not there
I shall cover my face

the daughter under the sheet
on the mortuary slab
is vowed to chastity and silence
the mother on the marble mattress in church
has lost her daughter, and has died in childbed
their shrouds, their wedding veils dissolve
into the salt swaddling bands of the sea

deep buried, the oyster sits
on the gravel bed men have dug for her
their fingers fret at her frilled
stone petticoats: they wish to culture her
her valves open in welcome; they insert grit
her valves close; our mouths bleed, and are full of
           rocks

the woman on the couch goes home
and reads the morning papers
in bed, the cave of her becoming
rolling her tongue over jagged words
she remembers the sea, her mother
she re-members herself, she is forced to become a poet
she is forced to bear witness, to defend herself
then from the injuries inflicted she creates pearls

investigation shows
the details of the injuries inflicted
were omitted at the first hearing
the decision to omit them had been taken
in order not to distress her father
because they were not relevant

knowledge of the body is not relevant?
but the body resurrects itself, and returns
home in a tin boat, borne across the sea
which stutters over and over
at jagged logical rocks
which interrupts the chatter of death
sentences with staccato pearls

at the first hearing of our words
our willingness to admit inside knowledge
to admit that we were there, that we were witnesses
that we could speak of it, caused much distress

the woman on the couch is much distressed
in order that the fathers may not be distressed

in order that
the pathologist, the surgeon, the policeman, the
          coroner
may have clean hands, may return home
to lie
between clean sheets, to dream of clean
daughters and filthy whores

This poem refers to the death of a young nurse, Helen Smith,
in mysterious and never fully explained circumstances,
in Saudi Arabia in 1983, and to the controversy at the inquest
on the cause of her death. Some of the lines of the poem
are lifted directly from newspaper reports of the case at the time.

that girl
with her sharp
hips, pelvic bones
pointed like sycamore
leaves, she
with her boy's crop, hair
cut short as stubble in the corn
fields where fire and smoke
begin, scarlet heaps of burning
that collapse softly to black ash

she unexpectedly
came running out
of darkness, past
the iron spears of railings
the rattle of shadows guarding the park

suddenly I remembered her: she
whom I lost, hidden
for years in mists like this one, a
shiver of silver along the street
september night arriving
cold and solid as a gun

after a decade of absence

frost on the pavement
edge, evening air a chilly
second skin, my mouth
open, the wind in my throat
desire quickening me

green and red lights
stream along the window
the street's an aquarium

black water outside our glass
submarine is streaked
through by silver eels

coral lamps twist up
flat strips of turquoise seaweed
line the pavement

orange goldfish
mouths blink
off–on

the bus noses the dark
rolls like a whale full
of many Jonases

later to be burped up
to float off
into the bigger maw of night

embroidery

the delicate hunt
the fingers cantering
glazed linen fields

a glossy hedge to leap
the silver stab
the red line pulling through

each stitch
is a beagle
with a bloody mouth

this green whip
steel blade
this tree divides the air in two

pressed round by stone
this tree grows up
the courtyard well

four floors fall past it
rain of books
a log-jam in my mind

Before this, I was sucking
at death's breast, gasping for more
whey as bitter as soot. I
gagged on spoonfuls of ash.

I paused, I gathered my skirts, raced upwards
dropping the world. I hung on and flew. To the
                dream city
I always believed in: true, though invisible
like the kingdom of God.

Down again. Crushed. I crawled the sidewalk grids
the repeated intersection strobe. Giants played
                Monopoly:
skyscrapers for dice, the green dollar bills of Central
                Park.
The food was fake, chic plastic suppers for dolls.

Everybody wanted so much, including me.
The rich ate the poor, then shat them into the subways
and the junkies' eyes were derelict lots, reflecting
the needles of syringe buildings poking at a lost skin.

Rescue. Down West Eleventh Street
a woman sat on her front
steps combing a cat. When she looked
at me I saw her black tadpole eyes.

She waved her fist, and the houses suddenly stopped.
She opened her palm and breathed
and the sky sprang up and out
uncreased, enormous, wholly blue. Her miracle.

The wind uncorked my mouth
and the Hudson river poured in.
I abandoned myself like a coat
and the river flowed through me.

We walked on the water, the salty wooden tongue
of the rotting pier, in a swarm of light.
She hugged herself like a secret sea:
'Once, here, we saw an albatross.'

In the cab cantering up Fifth Avenue, waltzing
from lane to lane with yellow grace
God sat beside me on the leatherette seat
and the driver sang to the wheel: 'go, baby, go.'

Along the New Jersey turnpike I rocked, straphanging
with both hands in the glass bus.
Oil refineries and trees streamed through my eyes and
        skin.
The hill of God inside and out. The end of me.

babysitting
(for Sarah)

October burns my stuttering tongue.
The sky is a warm whisky glass
that pours light, and the chestnut trees
are alive twice: glittering
domes that lift off, soft
explosions, rust and pink confetti
litter blurs the grass.

I wheel your son out, over
the grey breath of pavement
stencilled with the memory of plane leaves
soon to be frosted hard and white
as china plates. He fists
an arc of yellow plasticine:
'moon' he says: 'banana. Letter C.'

Later, from the train, I mark
the broken brown diamonds of fields
the black and white jigsaw of cows.
Illiterate, I can't decipher the waxy red
scrawl on the right-hand window, till the sun
suddenly prints it out, shadow-writing
on the opposite pane: 'beware: lovers at large.'

I remember how we played with the baby
rolling him, naked, to and fro between us
on your marital bed, like a cylindrical
seal I'd stamped with a new myth of
longing, belonging.

cold Catholicism. cut-price
white nylon virginity, filmy
meringue veils and crinolines
locked in cellophane boxes licked
by First Communicants.

I want a book
with leaves of glass, a stack
of transparencies. I imagine
rivers running along
the library shelves, a dictionary of rain.

scholarly sentences coffin me in crystal.
over and over
I hurl myself at invisible doors.
I cannot get in or out.
I cut myself, falling
down layers of stone lips.

I stammer scarlet onto white sheets. lace
and scallops. oysters in separate beds.
narcissi sprout on the pillow-cases.

the hooligan girl waves *no*, darting
with upflung hands from Apollo's grip.
her flesh shivers and splits. her belly
is sheathed in bark. she bursts
from her chrysalis with a heart
of wood. her fingertips and hair
are laurel wreaths.

I dreamed I wore a glass
dress. I took communion, chewed
and swallowed a stiff bunch of bay.
I spit out bitter and aromatic words.

1.
This morning, at nine,
opening the front door of our flat
onto the first-floor landing, I found
snow fallen in the house.

Silently, overnight, the stairs'
concertina angles were flattened
and smoothed out. No carpet but a
white drift between white walls.

The decorator trod in with
his glistening brushes, his tin
slopping cream paint. He swaddled the
banisters in cotton bandages, hushed me.

All afternoon I have been laying
new lino in the kitchen, its pattern
of white squares glossy as béchamel
flowing between my hands.

Snow is falling in me. My house
has splintered. This grief
can't be blotted by white dustsheets
or covered up by pearl vinyl.

2.

Above me that enormous silver mouth
mumbling on pins. A sort of aunt
counting her cross-stitch sewn
along the raw edges of sleep.

Night-boat pushes through darkness.
Cargo of tangled threads I try
in the morning to gloss into words.
This is the dream-work: to weave, to unweave.

My sisters learned to layer white
cotton for quilts, how to smock petticoats.
I pricked my finger, imagined, in coloured wools
a hessian garden where lovers kissed.

Why should I mend the torn linen sheets
of our bed, rip them in half, turn them
sides to middle, hem them again?
I make the best of everything I can.

Your absence undoes me.
I want to make, and make.
These days, I want to remain unfinished.
I need you to hear me out. To unravel me.

The anniversary

Mid December. Sky
cracks like caramel, brown
sugar grit shovelled
down streets of tossed laundry.
Pavements are pillows of ice.

Here is the runaway bed
on stilts that you made and
that I chose to lie in. Twin
effigies sulking in marble, hide
and seek kids in our wooden
horse, in our tree-house: now
we're wounded, in hospital.
Under our red woollen blanket
we twitch, don't touch.

I want to mend
what has been broken: our talk-
bone, our listening-bone.

This time I vow only
to see you clearly.

And I dream of our bed
as an ark, re-
borne down the city's
passages, as spring
melts the snows in a rush, to
the open sea. This is labour.
This time I take
a compass, an anchor, a chart.

Night starts at four o'clock. Under
my study window the street
soaks up the dark like scent
worn by a woman in rustling evening
dress, a scarf of shadow thrown
over her cold shoulders, her long gloves.
Gold squares, toy theatres, spring out opposite.

Going outside is necessary. A click
of the switch marks the spool
of film running, melts solid
certainties. Darkness surrounds me like
a bag my eyes pierce holes in. Milkily
the edges of vision dissolve, re-form.
The world shines in deep negative.

I am not stupid. I know how to act.
Disembodied, clouded by a great
tweed coat, I'm anonymous, a
white moon flickering past kerb-
crawlers like another fantasy,
unspotted by rapists (this time), fixing
policemen with my stone glance.

What's a nice girl like me
doing out alone in the fluent night
speeding past tarmac's ebony
glisten, the sealy bark
of plane trees, feet flying steady
as my heartbeat, the wind
behind streaming through me?

Night billows out in front of me like
black elastic. Mother doesn't hold me back.

The world is reversed. Gone into negative.
Pale monochrome of peaks, a white lid
on the lake, the valley newly scooped out
of white blocks then speckled with brown
grains. Pines bristle thinly
on the mountain's flank. Each black branch
is lined exactly with white like cut plush.
White fur paws of spruce trees.

We push up into steep woods. Our toecaps
cut steps in the blank ramp ahead. Walls
of snow plot the curve of the vanished
track. What were meadows are now full
wedges of white we plough across, knee-deep.
Behind us, our scribbles on winter's diagram.
Under our boots, the creak of snow's broken
crust; below that, the rustle of layers of manuscript.

The forest's a palimpsest, a folk-tale.
Some of its actors' names we recover from
fragile prints: hare, squirrel, fox, goat.
Others we guess at: this white blot might be
a badger's sett. Here is a magic tree
ribbed solid with icicles, dripping
candles of water. Here are white logs
laid out like dead brides.

Our narrator, the man in the red woollen cap
leads us to the myth's heart. He scrapes with his
stick in a white dip, exposes a perfect circle
of glazed grey ice. He uncovers the mirror
of the mother, she who goes away
comes back, goes away. Her cold eye blinks
unblinks. Our kiss on her round mouth is chalk,
inscribes us on her body's blackboard: want, want.

Next March, he tells us, all
the whiteness of these hills
will loosen, will slide off
like a nightdress, like a shroud.

Train journey Shrewsbury-Aberystwyth

Violet earth, green fuzz of grass.
Bright sticks fill the ditches, oildrums pile
next to a swamp rosy with pigs.

Under the elms, the graves are tidy bright
packets of seed laid out in a patience game.
The dead wear florals and do not care.

Snail churches crawl up the hills.
Sheep with red numbers stamped on their backs
lambs in black stockings, spill down the slope

fallen white petals. Chickens
scuttle and flap. Now the hills
swoop and leap, swell to mountains.

At every village stop, women and babies
are suddenly visible. The guardsvan disgorges
them, hung about with pushchairs and shopping.

The mothers have stood all the way
in the rattling dark. We rush away from them
as though we have taken vows

of freedom, instability, unchastity.
Single, as serious as brides
we hurtle towards the same deep bed.

On *Boulogne Sands*

(a painting by Philip Wilson Steer)

Le ciel est bleu.

Monique, the eldest, skinny and awkward in corsets, dark plait dropping straight as a plumb-line down her blue jacket, stares at the red and white striped bathing-machines. Stout men in navy wool splash in, the cold sea slopping over their shoulders. What is it like? She imagines a transformation total as baptism, her own voice crying out as she drowns. Today, being unwell, she is forbidden to swim.

La mer est vaste. Le soleil brille,

Frederique tucks up her scarlet skirt and white flounced petticoat, unpeels black stockings from legs creamy as stripped willow-sticks. She hops across the scooped-out hollows of the rocks, slipping on sopping green feathery moss, dips her feet into pools walled with limpets. Her heart is a pale crab jerking from side to side. She cocks an ear for the voices calling her back.

parmi les nuages blancs.

Marthe collects pebbles pale as eggs, smooth grey banded with charcoal and veined with mauve, speckled with glittery quartz. She picks up stiff dead starfish, seaweed in puckered rubber strips, parched and bleached cuttle-bones, mackerel-blue mussel shells opening like wings. Smuggled home in her pocket, the beach will lie under her in bed all night long. Glass waves rising and falling. Slither of water over dragged stones.

Il fait beau.

Chantal, the youngest, in a goffered white cotton sun-bonnet and pink smock, squats to prod the mound of sand she has dug, distended as Maman's belly. She carves out a moat in the wet sludge, then a shallow channel that runs to the edge of the sea. Connects them. Watches the cloudy waters rush in, surge and wash around the castle. Smash! she flattens it.

En vacances.

Lily Mount, the English governess, struggles to fill in the daily blank in her journal with halting French words. Her straw hat is looped with daisies and delphiniums, her pale hair puffed out at the sides. She would like to throw herself into the sea like a message in a bottle: save me. Soon it will be tea-time: lemonade in tin cups, fresh bread and bitter chocolate. The wind blows sand into her eyes, salt onto her lips.

Je voudrais. Je veux. Je manque de pratique.

We stumble up a ramp of air.
The rouged hostess dissolves
yellow grit and ice
in paper cups, doles out sweaty
fettucine, beef shavings in glue sauce.
The sky is blue as an apron.

The kitchen's clean machines
process the flesh coolly as hospitals.
Racks of knives and pans; fruit
and veg packed like wounds in gauze and ice.
Coffee beans in a glass jar: black
polished wooden beads that
slide through my hands, a broken rosary.
Our host invokes bones: risotto
with marrow, osso buco, boiled broth.
His wife hands ladles.

In the Faculty Club at nine
a silver lake of water in each glass, a
circular steel plaque, mirrors the
mouths of baby-faced men talking
business over breakfast: bacon
and weak white toast, eggs fried sunny side up.
Fresh soap and sausages. Fingers
of red blossom tap at the window pane.

The cafe is cut from onyx and formica, full
of purple neon striplights, indigo balloons.
Blue linen tablecloths, a metal counter
the waitresses re-spray
to polish off the marks of espresso cups.
Sunburned youths gobble sfogliatelle with ricotta
discuss real estate, singles computer dating parties
with silk-clad girl execs spooning in Sweet'n'Low.

I bite at a muffin stained with blueberries.
Fear of the future
breaks and enters me.